WHO'S IN CHARGE HERE? 1984

BY GERALD GARDNER

BANTAM BOOKS
TORONTO · NEW YORK · LONDON · SYDNEY · AUCKLAND

Dedicated to Harriet, Lindsay, and Joey
—still the greatest

WHO'S IN CHARGE HERE? 1984
A Bantam Book/July 1984

*Photographs courtesy of United Press International
and Wide World Photos, Inc.*

ISBN 0-553-34076-X

Published simultaneously in the United States and Canada

*Bantam Books are published by Bantam Books, Inc. Its trademark, consisting of the
words "Bantam Books" and the portrayal of a rooster, is Registered in the United
States Patent and Trademark Office and in other countries. Marca Registrada. Bantam
Books, Inc., 666 Fifth Avenue, New York, New York 10103.*

PRINTED IN THE UNITED STATES OF AMERICA

CW 0 9 8 7 6 5 4 3 2 1

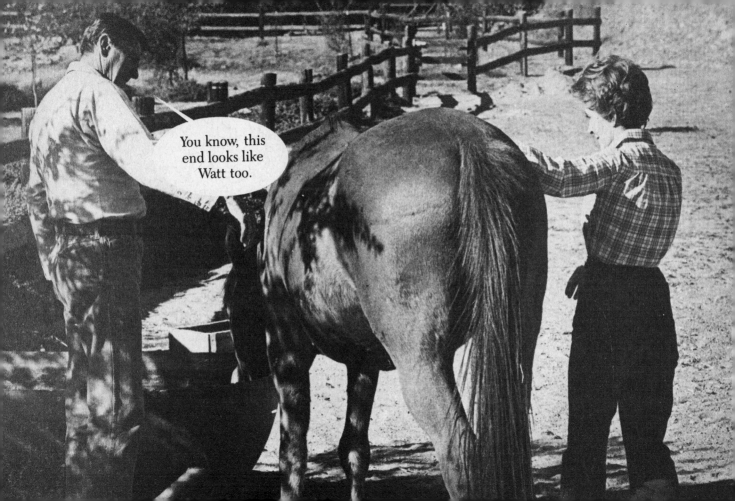

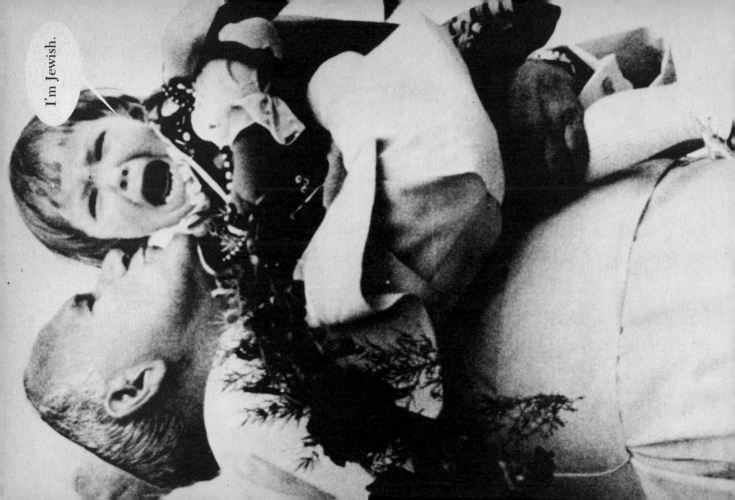

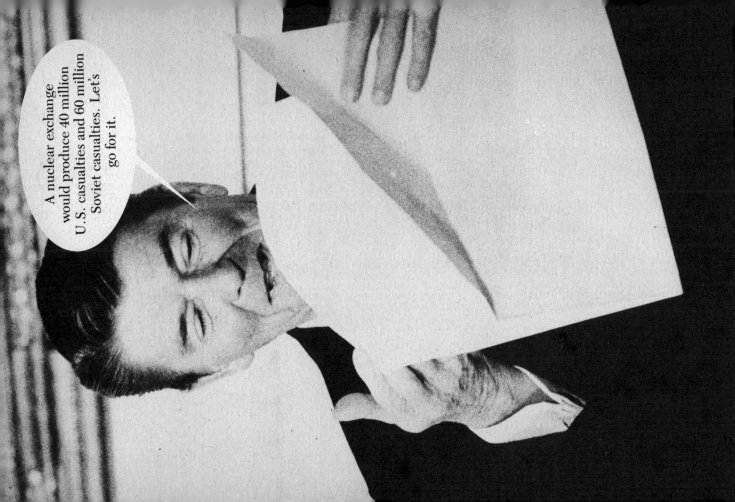

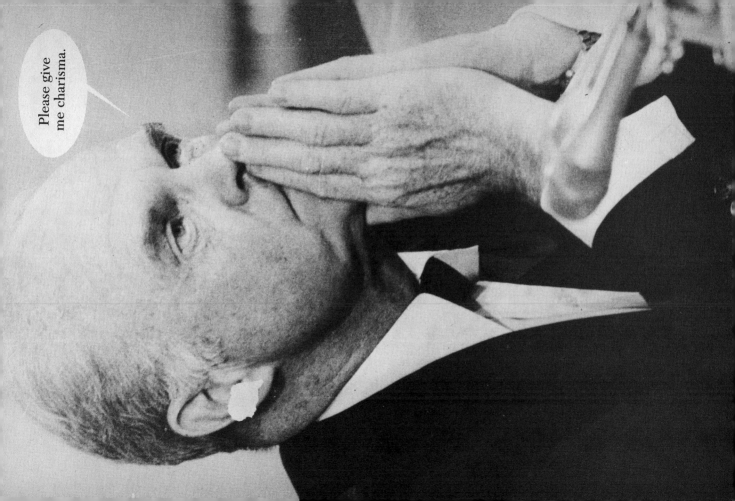

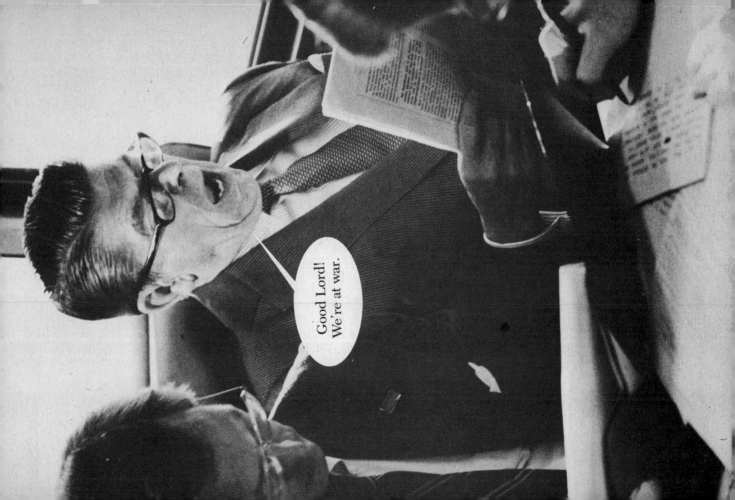

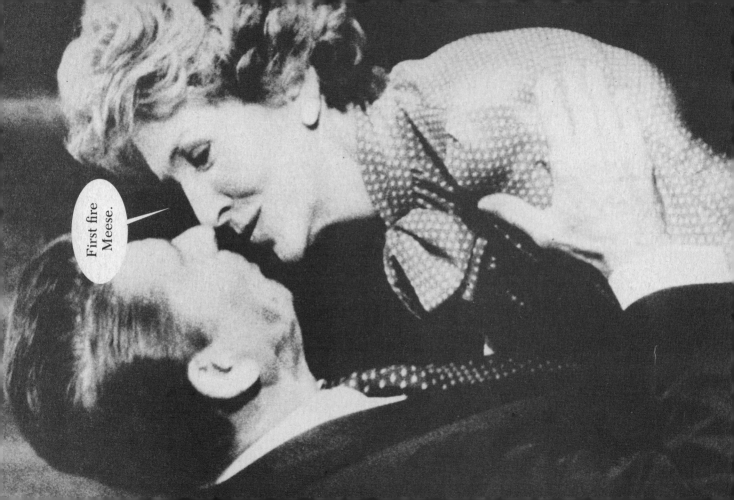

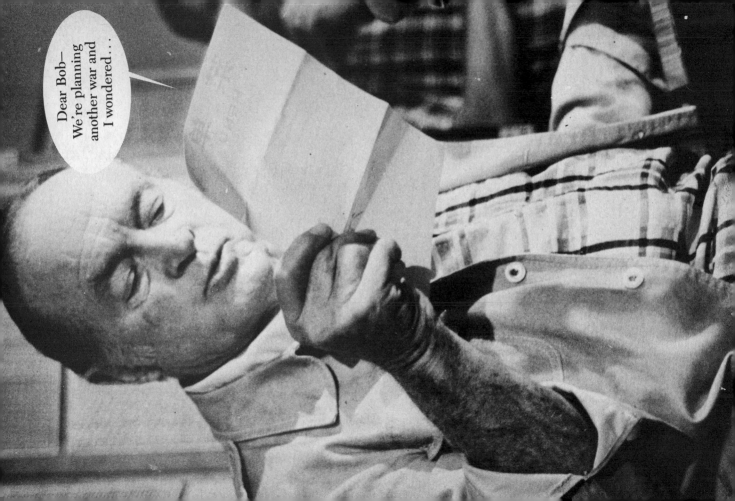

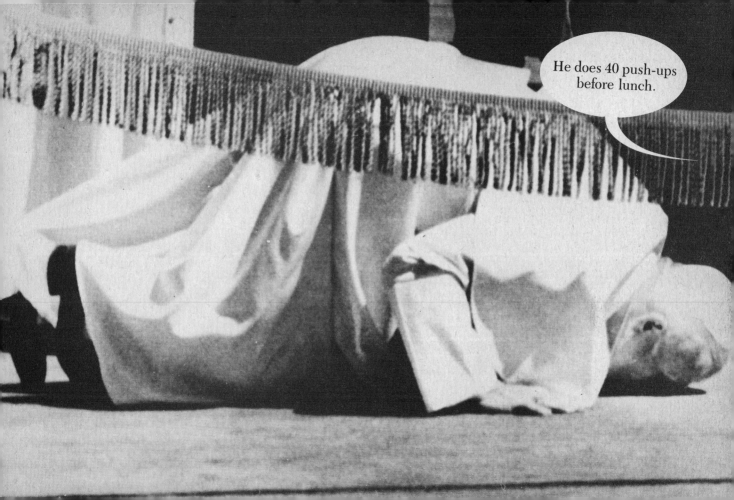

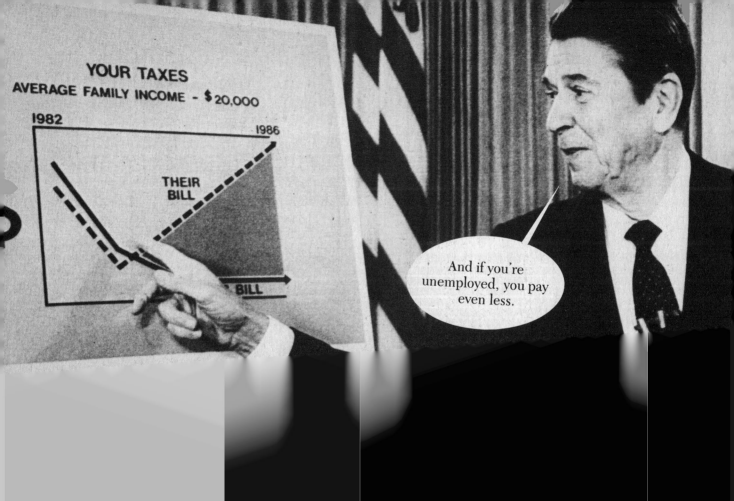

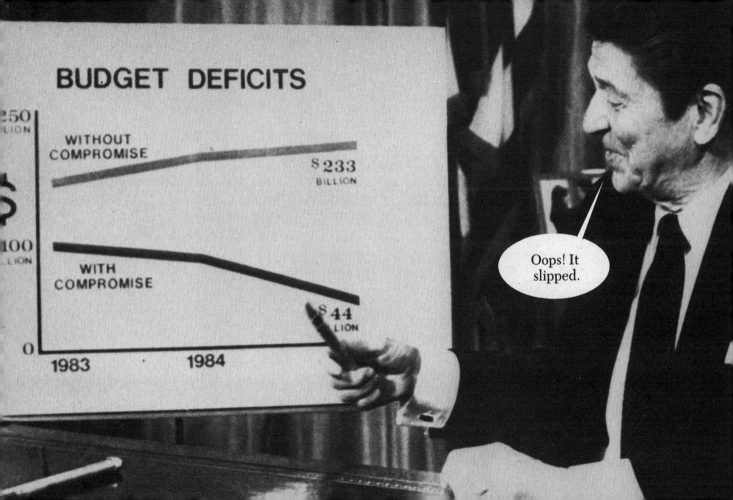

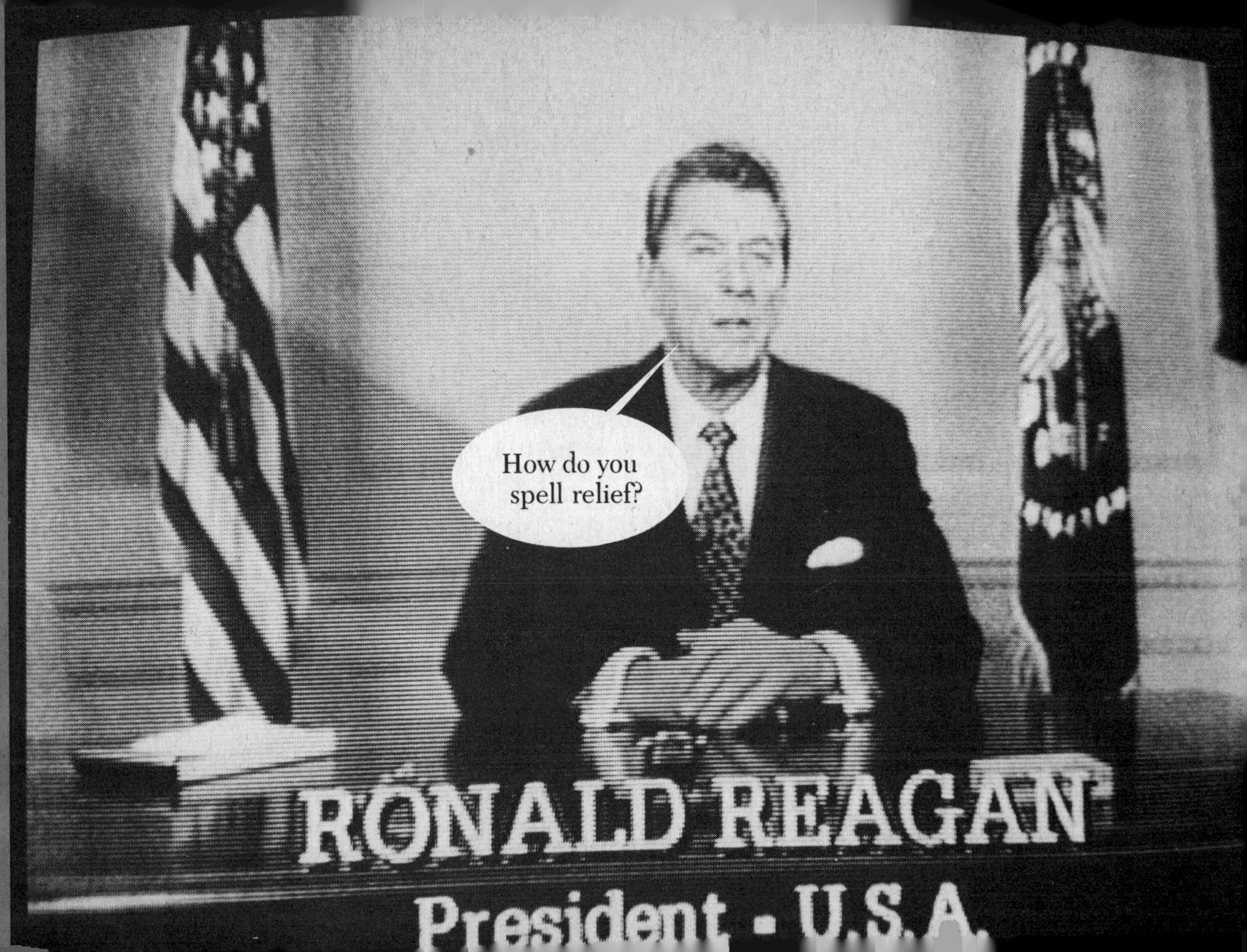
How do you spell relief?
RONALD REAGAN
President - U.S.A.